A Guide For

Developing Successful
Millennial Leaders

Scott Sadler

People ∞ Process ∞ Profit
www.creative-conflict-solutions.com
971-600-3856

ISBN-13: 978-06923048-8-4
ISBN-10: 0692304886

Published by:
Sadler Enterprises, LLC

Edited by:
Jennifer-Crystal Johnson
www.JenniferCrystalJohnson.com

Questions? Comments? Reach us at:
www.Creative-Conflict-Solutions.com
971-600-3856
scott@creative-conflict-solutions.com

Table of Contents

Introduction

Never in history has there been a more complicated time for business leadership with the most expensive and important asset in business: human capital. The instant information age has *not* provided solutions to problems in the workforce and, in fact, has sometimes created false beliefs about people, expectations, and experience.

Facts:

- Never in history have there been five generations in the workforce at the same time!
- Never in history has there been a more influential generation than the Millennials or, if you prefer, Gen Y.
- Never in history has there been so much danger in losing institutional knowledge in organizations as generations retire and others advance.
- Never in history has there been a better time to connect with, and create success from, so many different viewpoints on life and business. We need only listen....

We are living in a very dynamic age. Instant information, instant gratification, and real-time details are being posted to the world in life and in business. This is vastly different from how previous generations were raised. The adjustments of the older worker to the perceived impatience from a younger generation create a turbulent devil's punchbowl of misunderstandings, communication barriers, hurt feelings, lack of respect, and disconnect.

Business leaders, human resource people, and department managers trying to keep it all together among these different factions find that it is becoming more challenging each day. The hours spent on keeping these generations working as an effective team has become so intrusive to the core focus of a business that many of these business leaders are not sure what the main focus of their jobs really is anymore. This is no longer a distraction; it is a very big issue that is here to stay. It is becoming the new normal.

Currently, in late 2014, the Millennial generation is the largest demographic at 27% of the workforce in the United States. This number is expected to be 50% by 2020! This, coupled with Baby Boomers retiring at a rapid pace, and advancement expectations of many Millennials that are not realistic in the minds of many business leaders, is creating a tidal wave of problems on an epic scale. This is not only an issue in the US, but also for every country on the planet. We must acknowledge the fact that our lifestyles are changing, business models are changing, and we as leaders must change. We must be able to communicate the need for these changes and what they mean with respect to each generation and their unique contributions to the world.

See the chart below to familiarize yourself with the ages of each generation. This is a general guideline and many studies show a slightly different span of years to depict the different generations.

	Silent Generation	Baby Boomers	Generation X	Generation Y	Generation Z
Birth Year	1922-1945	1946-1964	1965-1978	1979-2000	2001-
Age in 2014	92-69	68-51	49-36	35-14	13-

Chapter 1:

Engage

> *"Every relationship lives or dies one conversation at a time."*
>
> *~Susan Scott, Author, Fierce Conversations*

How do you engage your people? As an Executive Coach this is one of the first questions I ask a client when they bring me into their business. This one question can lead to solutions in leadership issues, production or operational effectiveness, marketing and customer retention, interpersonal skills, etc. Many business leaders cannot see the correlation between people engagement and other aspects of the business. I understand because I have lived it and learned from it in my own businesses.

As business leaders, we are faced with a myriad of barriers to success, both personally and professionally. We are stretched in multiple directions at once and expected to set the example of how to perform and succeed. It can be easy to delegate incorrectly or have unrealistic expectations of our people, especially when we are overwhelmed with the many challenges of operating a business. In other words, we sometimes put people last. It is my intention to help people focus on the *Human* in Human Capital.

To do this we must understand the belief systems of people and how those influences infiltrate the workplace. By no means am I suggesting we become counselors or psychologists! People need to own their own personal issues on the job. However, when we elevate to the ten thousand foot view of the people in our operation, we can start identifying trends, habits, and issues more easily. More of this view comes up in the next chapter.

The process of engagement is about a mindful plan with its sole purpose being to guide interactions with Millennials, beginning in the recruitment process. This in no way means you are going to be unethical or show favoritism to one generation over another by using different processes. There needs to be one process for all. As Boomers retire and more Millennials join the workforce or advance in leadership, the approach must change as well. Changing the approach to hiring and training is something that corporations and entrepreneurs have not always accepted. "If it isn't broke, don't fix it," no longer applies.

Engage early in the process by talking to your potential team members in 3-, 6-, and 12-month expectations. If you charge out of the gate talking about how it will look for them in 15 or 20 years you may lose them, as statistics show a trend away from the tradition to begin and end a career with one company. Many do want to know about long-term opportunities in the first two interviews, but in my experience it is best to ask them what they want to know and let them guide the conversation. This will allow you to know where they are coming from and what they are expecting and thinking about for their career path and life.

If you have short-term opportunities for advancement, be very clear about the steps to advance and let them know what the support looks like to help them move ahead. If you have not had a clearly defined advancement outline for previous generations, be prepared to discuss it with other generations who may view this as favoritism. "We did it this way so they should, too," is always the most popular water cooler conversation and the most common reason for disconnect between generations in the workplace.

I have found it helpful to include other generations from many different departments in the discussion from the very beginning. Pose questions such as, "If you were to move up the ladder again, what resources would you like to see available to you that you did not have then?" or, "If you were to teach someone how to do your job and advance in the company, how you would you lay it out for them now that you have been through it yourself?"

By engaging with the other generations, you will bring a powerful synergy to the process that can create great benefits for your organization in the form of mentorship, knowledge transfer, and a collaborative culture.

Chapter 2:

Mentor

> *"Surround yourself only with people who will lift you higher."*
>
> *~Oprah Winfrey*

I can already hear the collective groan. Millennials have said it over and over again: "I need mentoring." There are many reasons for the need for mentoring and I have listed a few below:

- Helicopter parenting
- Desire to advance in a company rapidly
- Having a strong desire for instant information from a reliable source

We have heard or experienced firsthand the stories of the demanding Millennials and their overbearing parents. While I know there are some of those, I am not convinced that an entire generation can, or should, be so labeled.

It is up to us as leaders to recognize talent, encourage and support development of that talent, and create our future leaders on a case by case basis. Doing so requires us to step back for a better view and understand how these times are different than when we were in their position. This may mean we have to re-prioritize what we do each day or week as leaders. It may demand connecting to our teams as *the* priority. We may need to create an open forum for your people to share ideas or concerns with upper management. Notice I say *share,* which is much different than implementing said ideas.

I would like to address the *Helicopter Parent* topic for a moment. In order to understand the issue of some of our young applicants and team members, we need to go back a generation or two.

Boomer parents had Gen X children. For many Boomer parents, including my own, both held jobs outside of the home. It was the first generation that had an "epidemic" of both parents being at work when kids got home from school. As children, Generation X, or the *Slacker Generation,* had to learn to deal with becoming independent more quickly. This sometimes led to poor decision making with bigger consequences than if a parental figure had been present.

As Gen X'ers matured and began to have kids of our own, we were able to use the gift of hindsight and study the way we were raised. Some of us decided it would be different for our kids. We, in a sense, were going to make sure to make up for those things missing in our childhood with our kids. This then led to some *over-parenting* in which self-esteem was the main priority. No winners and losers, everyone gets a prize, and there are celebrations and graduations for anything and everything. When you look at this now as Millennials enter the workforce, coupled with a struggling economy over the last decade, it is no surprise that kids are living at home - sometimes until they are 30 years old.

When they get to the workplace, they may see authority figures as they saw their parents: best friend, cheerleader, and rescuer. Like it or not, as business leaders, we need to teach a different way to these individuals. Our leadership style, organization, and the Millennials must adapt, which we will discuss in the next chapter.

Mentoring can take on many forms in an organization. It begins with a conversation. As a management team, ask yourselves the tough questions.

- Are we doing everything we can to ensure our Millennials will succeed, or are we putting them in the flow of business without a life jacket?
- What can this support look like and how much time will it take away from other projects?

It is sometimes quite helpful to bring in a third party executive coach to do a 360 degree assessment with your entire team to acquire the feedback you need to make powerful changes.

If you are a C-Suite Executive, consider having a monthly forum either in person or online that focuses on answering questions from the Millennial staff (and others, of course) that pertain to the company and their place in it, in groups or one-on-one, depending on your situation.

If you are a department manager, in human resources, or in any position working side by side with younger staff members, it would pay dividends to put together a thoughtful plan for mentoring and coaching your people each day. In business, we tend to leave mentoring out of our planning. The reality is that it affects all the other areas we *do* plan for: financial, operations, sales, and marketing. It our people do not feel cared for, if they do not have access to someone who can answer their questions or teach them about the company culture, they are going to find someone who speaks to these needs – most likely in another company.

Another major benefit of mentoring new, younger employees is that you can develop a systematic knowledge transfer plan. In most organizations, the Baby Boomers and the Silent Generation are retiring and taking with them critical institutional knowledge that cannot be learned except in one of two ways:

1) By putting in the years to learn the things they know, or

2) By the people who *have* put in the years teaching this knowledge to others.

Option two is preferable since it saves a lot of money in productivity and training costs and the Millennial gets the desired mentoring. As an added bonus, most of those mentors feel valued in a way they may never have before.

This institutional knowledge is not in training manuals or in a policy or procedure book. This knowledge is the meaty stuff you simply know from doing your job well for many years. Many of these folks don't even know that they know it! You may have to coach it out of them, job shadow and document what they do to get it, and then you may have to teach them how to teach it to others.

Here in my hometown of Salem, Oregon our community college, Chemeketa, and our economic development agency, SEDCOR, collaborated to develop the Industrial Maintenance Operator/Mechanic Training Program (or IMOM) project and were the winners of the 2009 Collaborative Partnership award.

This program was developed to provide the Salem region with an industry-driven workforce training program designed to advance the talent capabilities of existing employees and effectively transfer the knowledge and expertise of a seasoned workforce to the next generation of workers. The goal of the IMOM program is to become a model not only to prepare the next generation of replacement workforce, but also to stabilize the regional workforce needs, resulting in accelerating the Salem region's strategic global competitiveness. Chemeketa Community College trained the experienced workers on how to teach their institutional knowledge and train the younger workers; SEDCOR identified and provided support for those manufacturers and others who were facing the loss of this invaluable knowledge.

It would be invaluable for you to implement this type of program for your company's Millennials, Generation X, and Boomers. Win, win, win.

Action Items:

What is the average age of the human capital in my organization?

_____

What is the quality of the conversations in our workplace? Are they meaningful? Is there a planned outcome with accountability? How can they be improved?

_____
_____
_____
_____
_____
_____

List the top three improvements you would like to see overall with your human capital:

1. _____
2. _____
3. _____

People ∞ Process ∞ Profit
www.creative-conflict-solutions.com
971-600-3856

Chapter 3:

Culture

> *"There is nothing more difficult to take in hand, more perilous to conduct, or more uncertain in its success, than to take the lead in the introduction of a new order of things."*
>
> *~ Niccolo Machiavelli*

Organizational culture is highly underrated on the list of priorities for many business leaders until there is a crisis with their people. Great cultures begin with the decision to *have* a culture. Understanding how the different generations are a part of it is a small piece of this best practice.

In a recent survey of adults age 18-24, 55% put finding a job they love as their top priority, while 22% were seeking a well-paying job. If you set your target to creating a culture that was in alignment with your people's passion or their values and pay them well, according to this survey, you would be appealing to 77% of the marketplace for new hires and retain the staff you have far more easily.

Human beings seek happiness. If we boil it down, from the time we are born until the time we die, we are constantly seeking happiness in one form or another. It is when our need to be happy is not met or we believe we cannot be happy that many problems begin and suffering deepens in our lives.

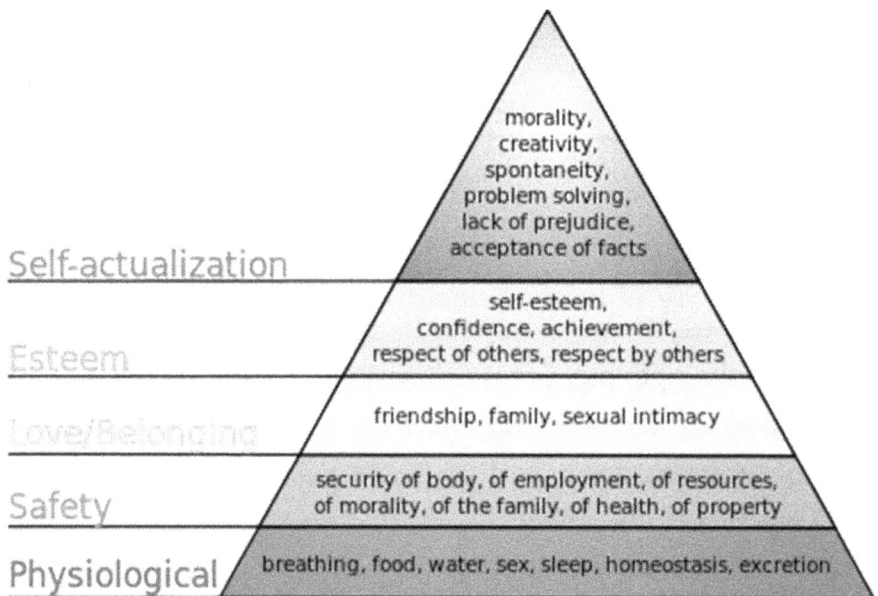

Maslow's hierarchy of needs shown above is an excellent tool for every business leader and entrepreneur to understanding order to plan for and execute a happy and highly successful organizational cultural plan.

As business leaders, we impact the safety stage in the lives of others, and they in turn can impact the safety stage in our own. At times this can prove to be difficult. It is especially difficult to reconcile for a small business owner who may be struggling to get a business off the ground and attempting to solve his or her own safety needs while attempting to meet those needs for the staff. A strong outline for the vision for the organization can be very helpful as a guide to attracting, retaining, and/or removing people who are not a good fit for an organization.

I once had a client I will call Bob (not his real name). Bob was President and CEO of his own manufacturing company that employed two management team members and between 10 and 16 production workers at any given time. We worked on a variety of things together for his company growth and systemization. One of the main focuses was on his company's cultural identity. There was no real or thoughtful planning around his vision.

His best production worker, who handled a very labor-intensive position, had some real issues. Her safety needs were not being met outside of the job. This led to many serious disruptions in the workplace, including threats of violence against her supervisor. Bob, the CEO, did nothing. He was not open to termination or to any other serious disciplinary actions. His worry about losing his "specialist" had won over his 30,000-foot view of the culture as a whole. Other workers felt slighted because they were working hard and not causing issues, so when no repercussion came from her actions they began to wonder why they tried so hard. The supervisor was really upset. Her suggestions for discipline were not heard (nor were mine) and as far as I know this person is still employed there. This is a case where one employee and weak leadership were allowed to set the tone in the work culture. The employees should always have a voice in the work culture, but leadership needs to make decisions to show they support the culture, and many times firing is as important as hiring.

Bob's lack of effort in creating a mindful plan for culture ahead of time, coupled with the mishandling of a rogue employee, undermined his supervisor and showed the rest of the staff there was no consistency in dealing with people or circumstances within the company. The safety stage has to work both ways for the employer and the employees.

In another situation, Jeff (again, not his real name), the president of a company, called me to discuss ways to improve the culture in his organization. He owned a small business to business service company employing 15 people. Jeff had put the culture first in his planning. He had it in mind when he hired and fired, but more importantly, he was very interested in diversity, new ideas, and asked everyone to challenge the status-quo. Still, he felt a bit stagnant.

Together we came up with some ways to improve the culture even more. Jeff started sharing some of the business financial information in staff meetings, encouraging others to ask questions and make suggestions. When it was time to consider hiring, many of the staff asked if it would not be better to split some of the work and save the cost of a new person. They were now able to think like owners and make great business decisions. I know not every business will share financial information. I have done so in my businesses and found it to be a way to build trust, while educating my teams about how a business operates. This always led to a better-educated decision making process.

The other thing Jeff and I did was implement two types of meetings. The "big idea" meetings were a sit-down for everyone to share their latest thoughts and ideas for any area of the business. This was a creative problem solving time and not just a "talk about it and do nothing" kind of meeting. It occurred once per week.

The second meeting was for 20 minutes each morning with key people. This was a stand-up meeting right at 8:00 AM and it consisted of a daily update on projects and progress.

This was meant to be a quick, down and dirty report in which each person got five minutes to share and then went on with their day.

The benefits that Jeff has received are much more than he had hoped for. He is currently planning his exit strategy and his team is very supportive and excited about their role in the company in the future. Meanwhile they still have their business issues, people issues, etc., but are in a much better position to deal with them and move on than many other companies due to the president's commitment to create an *intentional* culture rather than hoping for the best.

Building a positive, supportive culture also allows you to use this as a recruiting advantage. There are many companies who do this very well; Google, Starbucks, and Twitter are always on the Forbes 100 best places to work list. Number 21 on the list for 2014 is a company I have had the pleasure to do some work for, the Kimpton Hotel and Restaurant Group. This organization has a culture that includes:

- Rewarding hard work
- Enjoyable co-workers
- Celebrations of anything they deem relevant
- Continuing education
- Advancement from within

- Travel
- An overall feeling of being a part of something bigger

They are a hip, growing company that excels in recruitment of the right employees, and that same culture is how they approach customer service. No detail is ignored, and the competition is certainly taking notice.

Take an objective look at your work environment. Can it be better? What would you do to make it a more relaxed place to be for your team without losing sight of the work everyone is there to do? Some studies suggest we spend 80-85% of our time at work with our co-workers. Doesn't it make sense to work in a culture that is creative and energized so people *want* to be there every day?

Make it your goal to contribute less to the $360 billion in turnover cost last year. The foundation for recruiting the right people, reducing your turnover, and earning more profits begins by creating a great place where people want to be.

Chapter 4:

Coaching

> *"A coach is someone who tells you what you don't want to hear, who has you see what you don't want to see, so you can be who you have always known you could be."*
>
> *~ Tom Landry*

When I conduct workshops on coaching as a leadership skill, one of the first things I acknowledge is the overuse of the word "coaching" in a professional context. When coaching for business leaders first began in the 1980s, many people believed it to be a passing fad and consultants scoffed at the idea of this "feel good" scam. The reality of the situation is people have been coached in business since the beginning of time. Taking the skills these leaders used and applying them with laser-like focus can produce amazing results in personal and professional growth. As coaching entered the new millennium, those results started to build and build into an industry that has experienced massive growth.

The proof is in the numbers. Sherpa Coaching reports the status and trends of the global coaching industry. In 2014, they reported the highest revenues to date for coaches and the demand took a significant leap. Today there are over 80,000 coaches worldwide, generating revenues that total nearly three billion dollars.

Coaching in the workplace addresses behavioral change for a culture, team, or individual. In my business, _Creative Conflict Solutions_, as with my colleagues at _Executive Coaching University_, we believe in _Values-Based Coaching_. Once you understand someone's values, you can begin to help him/her achieve a goal and overcome a barrier in alignment with those values in a way that has more sustainable results for the future.

Mentoring differs from coaching in that mentoring is showing someone the way things should be done and providing support to that end, while coaching is a co-creative process in which both parties bring equal value to the relationship toward a goal for the one being coached. Furthermore, coaching encourages problem-solving like nothing else. Depending on what's needed, the hybrid between mentoring and coaching is optimal in many situations.

Coaching effectively requires practice. One of the best things you can do to learn how to be an excellent coach is to hire a coach and work through anything that is holding you back, or toward a goal you have in mind. One note about hiring a coach: be sure your coach *has* a coach! Make sure they are practicing what they preach.

Coaching is conversation-based. Being an excellent coach requires possessing high level listening skills. This provides the ability to guide the one being coached to his or her desired outcomes, sometimes in spite of the person's resistance to change! Consider the fact that there are very few occasions for us, as busy people, to be simply heard by another person, free of judgment or distraction. This one benefit leads to trust, and where there is trust, amazing work can be done for an individual, team, and organization. As Coach Drayton Boylston says, "Coaching is the cure for this crisis."

Coaching is an art and a science. The science in how the brain works links very nicely with coaching, changing behaviors, and creating the discipline to sustain those changes at the source – the brain – for higher success rates in coaching than ever before.

The art comes in from practice, empathy, toughness, and a clear goal with each person being coached. The agenda is never ours. In companies this sometimes seems to be impossible when you need Millennial Sally to perform better in her department. By approaching Sally with coaching as an option, you will have a better chance to create new behaviors than if you were to simply begin the disciplinary process for poor work performance.

Coaching addresses a person first and performance second. Sometimes in the process, the individual being coached suddenly realizes they are not meant for the kind of work they are doing or the position they are in. This is an excellent opportunity to move them to a different position, or they may leave the company and you can find someone who is a better fit for you. It is best to be proactive in a conversational setting whenever possible. As mentioned earlier, the average Millennial will have 20 jobs in their lifetime.

As business leaders we must incorporate a more consistent coaching approach than ever before to reduce our turnover costs and increase employee engagement and trust, which leads to happier people and higher profits. Win-win.

Action Items:

How can we, as a leadership team, develop more of a coaching management style?

_____

_____

_____

How much are we _really_ listening to our managers and staff? What action do we take that shows they are being heard?

_____

_____

_____

List the top three improvements you would like to see with your communication process:

1. _____

2. _____

3. _____

Chapter 5:

Entitled or Enlightened?

> *"Change is, change does, change has, and change always will be, may as well embrace it!"*
>
> *~ Unknown*

It has been said Millennials are the "entitlement" generation or the "me "generation. The more research I do, the more I am convinced that this is inaccurate. I see the Millennials as an exciting beginning of positive change. Yes, there are some clear and distinct differences between Generation X and the Boomers; no doubt about it.

There was also a major difference between my grandmother and me in our age and experiences. I was fascinated by her views that had been formed growing up in the depression and WWII. She and others in her generation were dealing with the things that so many of us living in the United States rarely have to deal with today. She had judgments and opinions that I did not agree with, and I had my own young views on the world that she did not agree with. My favorite thing to do was to sit with her in her dining room over coffee and toast and have these quiet discussions on the world before, the world now, and the world we envisioned in the future. We had enough love and respect for each other to listen and learn from one another.

As we move toward handing the leadership of our business, community, countries, and – indeed – the *world* to the soon-to-be largest generation in history, we must learn to bridge the gap to see the value each generation brings. Change is happening, rapid change can be devastating, and we must find the balance. The balance comes from asking the right questions and listening to the answers.

It is important to view the world through someone else's lens for a while and honor the other person's experiences as being real and having validity. Different is never wrong, it is only different.

Boomers live to work, Gen X work to live, and Millennials live and then work.

Born between 1976 and 2001, this generation is predicted to be 36% of our entire workforce in the US and Canada by 2014 and almost 50% by 2020. By comparison, Gen Xers represent only 16% of the workforce.

What makes this important? Many of you may already see the results of leading this seemingly disconnected group of young people. It has been reported that the average Millennial will have 20 jobs over their lifetime. This means every 24-36 months, we can plan on replacing this individual right about the time he/she is fully integrated into our operation. The turnover costs for companies will be out of control if this trend continues.

Understanding how this generation sees the world will be critical for companies to embrace this sometimes misunderstood group. As Baby Boomers continue to retire, employers are facing a major gap in leadership. Attracting top talent from the Millennials will require changes in how a company engages these workers.

Here are a few points to consider:

- 47% of Millennials tend to favor working for smaller businesses of 100 or fewer employees and 30% for businesses of 100-500 employees. Only 23% work for larger companies according to Payscales "GenY on the Job" report. Many are entrepreneurs.
- Creating an environment of open communication in your companies' culture is important. Millennials need to be heard and have a way to provide input. Providing systematic, routine ways to engage them will make a big difference and will provide you with some exciting new ideas you may have missed otherwise.

- Providing mentoring will be well received as your veteran Boomers retire. Millennials are sponges eager for information. Providing mentoring in leadership will be a good investment that can provide excellent returns.
- Provide a sense of purpose. Being of value is critical, not just for your organization but also for them to be in alignment with their own values. Global Social Consciousness is a way of life for this generation and those companies that integrate it into their culture will be ahead of the curve for retaining employees longer.
- It is imperative to accept technology as part and parcel of this generation. You can use this to your advantage in your companies even if you are not fully up to speed in the latest trends in social media, advertising, or software. These young people have never known a world without technology. Put them in a position to utilize this skill set and both of you will be happier for it.

Having volunteered for the past eight years in a Leadership Youth Program, I can attest to the highly intelligent, motivated young people in our communities and businesses. The real question is how, as business owners, we will accommodate the way they see the world to maintain our effectiveness and profits in our companies. Prepare for the change. It is upon us now.

Are Millennials Bringing You to Tears?

When asked at a corporate retreat to detail his biggest challenge as a senior level executive, an esteemed colleague recently shared with me that he was literally brought to tears of frustration as he described his efforts to connect and inspire his younger workforce.

Turnover from this segment was at an all-time high and it was severely affecting morale, production, and leadership.

This scenario is happening all over the world as the Millennials represent 30% of our workforce and will be over 40% by 2020. The press has written about this generation as the "me generation." There are more similarities in values than one may think between generations; it is the *order* and priorities of using these values in their lives that are different.

Here are three suggestions to engage differently with your Millennial workforce. If you want to gain a competitive edge and reduce turnover costs and your frustration, keep reading!

- Create a plan. Seek outside expertise if necessary to create a strategic approach to this human capital issue. Address it like a budget issue, capital project, operational issue, or other business system. Also, please include your Human Resource people but remember – this is a leadership issue, not an HR issue.

- Ask your Millennials to weigh in. Get a better understanding of what the expectations are from your people. Asking during an exit interview is too late to salvage your investment in that person, so be proactive! Many times the solutions are within an organization. All we must do is ask for it.

- This is a worldwide epidemic in business as more Boomers retire and Millennials move in to fill the ranks. Coaching as a management style has never been more important than it is right now. Seek coach training for your leaders and begin to transform your culture to create buzz with Millennials as an organization that "gets it." This requires a different mindset in how we lead. Having a coaching professional to help see things differently and ask provocative questions of the entire organization stimulates new thinking, which leads to quicker solutions. All business problems are people problems.

It is a new world. It is changing rapidly. It will not be "the way it was" ever again. By acknowledging these things and creating a plan to engage Millennials differently, you will be out in front as the trend-setter with this vital workforce and future leaders. Your turnover costs will drop and company morale will rise, not to mention your life will get a whole lot better when you are not frustrated to tears.

Three More Things You Can Do to Reduce Turnover of Gen Y

Companies must adapt to the workforce and what they are looking for if they hope to reduce costs associated with loss of productivity and turnover. Millennials are always looking for growth opportunities, so why not make them available in your own firm? Here are some ideas to get you thinking about how to begin.

1) **They want to have input.** Only 23% of all Millennials will go to work for major corporations. They are more interested in smaller companies and having more input in their work. They are not interested working in a cubicle and going home only to come in and do it again. It is imperative to create an "intrepreneurship" (entrepreneurial way to operate with*in* an organization) culture as a way for them to express the entrepreneurial qualities they possess.

2) **Lifestyle Flexibility.** Create a workplace flex program. Harvard Business Review August 2012 reports that remote workers are more engaged.

They tend to work longer hours, are more focused with fewer distractions, and generally have better communications with fellow staff and supervisors. Kenneth Matos, senior director of employment research and practice at the Families and Work Institute, says it best, "Think of work-flex as a dynamic partnership between employers and employees that defines how, when, and where work gets done in ways that work for all – including families, clients, and communities."

3) **Promote from within.** It sounds obvious, right? This is an ongoing process of preparation of your human capital with cross training, coaching, and communication about how the organization operates as a whole. As leaders, our motivation comes from the fact that it costs us 1.7 times more to hire externally rather than promote from within. For the Millennial worker, it means they are getting the mentorship and growth opportunities that will keep them engaged for years to come.

Time for a Millennial Makeover

As business owners, we are always looking for the edge. Many of us are looking for ways to get ahead of our competition, keep up with what our consumers demand, and create a viable workforce.

Most of us in labor intensive businesses would agree that one of the most challenging things we must find balance with is our people, or the human capital, in an organization. It has been said that any business problem is a people problem. That has never rung more true than now.

As Boomers are retiring rapidly, companies are seeking to backfill the positions vacated with the Gen Y population or Millennials. Millennials represent 25% of American workers, according to the US Bureau of Labor Statistics. By 2020, that number will grow to more than 40%. The oldest members of the generation are turning 30 this year, the beginning of their most productive work years.

What is the problem? Millennials view the world differently than any previous generation before it.

Here are a few characteristics you may have noticed:

- They tend to be very socially conscious and expect their employer to be as well. I had a millennial client who recently left his management job – where he made a good living – to go to work for a competitor for less money who was more in alignment with his personal beliefs and world views.

- Millennials ask a lot of questions and want to have a voice in the decision making process. They want to work for more than the money.

- They are not afraid to make changes and can be somewhat impatient. They will make changes quickly if it serves their goals or if their employer seems disinterested in them.

- Recent studies indicate that Millennials favor smaller businesses. According to a 2012 report by *Payscale*, 47% of Millennials in the workforce are employed by small businesses of 100 or fewer employees and 30% for businesses of 100-500 employees. Only 23% work for larger companies and many are entrepreneurs.

Seeing how the average Millennials will have 20 jobs over their lifetime tells us we have to make some significant changes to how we hire and retain our best people. Some reports show that average turnover costs can be as high as $24,000 per person! Another thing to consider is that employers will be facing leadership gaps as the increasing retirement of Baby Boomers continues. To develop those leaders and retain them, companies must change their approach to hiring them. Potential employees are now interviewing companies as much or more than the companies are interviewing them.

Three tips to get you started:

- Get an outsider's perspective of your current culture and identify where you need to improve and what you are already doing well. Hire someone with deep listening skills and business leadership experience for best results.

- Ask Millennials outside of your organization and within it what they look for and expect from an employer, and if at all possible, craft your offerings around the answers you receive. For example, flexible work time, round table discussion groups, and adding value to the community and the world are three great places to begin.

- Don't underestimate the importance of integrating soft skill training into your company culture. Coaching as a management style and encouraging authentic communication protocols would be a great start that will resonate with the younger generation.

Annual turnover costs have been estimated at 416 billion dollars in the US. With turnover at an all-time high, this is decreasing efficiencies and shrinking profits. This can cripple a business on the edge and create long-term issues for those currently doing well.

It is time to decide how we will accommodate the millennial generation in our businesses and develop the future with them. This is not just an HR issue that they can "figure out." It is a leadership issue that should be moved to the top of the "to do" list.

Three Things You May Not Know About Millennials

Every day I work with employers and their human capital. The challenges of hiring and retaining Millennials are becoming a common theme with many of them. The world is changing faster than ever before. There are some individuals and companies who want to freeze-frame a particular place in time and space, and it is from this place their beliefs and values are drawn.

We have all heard that change is the only consistent thing in life, which is true, except we do not always welcome it when it arrives. This is a major difference between the Millennials' viewpoint on life and business as opposed to that of other generations. For the most part they welcome change, but are quite present and in the moment when it occurs, taking it all in stride and seeking the opportunity that is to come from it.

Did You Know?

1. *Millennials put the focus on **being** before **doing***. They want whatever they have to do to be in a supporting role for being. Essentially what this means is they do not see the point of doing a task if it does not serve a bigger purpose on the level of spirituality, relationships, or planet consciousness. A recent study suggest Generation X, which is my generation, tried to achieve work-life

balance, whereas Millennials are demanding it, with three out of four surveyed saying that work-life issues drives their career choices. Corporate America, are you listening?

2. *Millennials are tech dependent.* Some report that this generation is the most tech savvy generation. This may be true, but I recently heard a speaker about this generation who believes they are tech *dependent* rather than tech savvy because they have grown up with the rapid technological changes of the 80s and 90s. Older generations may say publicly that we do not get it, but when something goes wrong with our iPhone or we cannot figure out Facebook, we call a Millennial! This ability to learn new technology, and enjoy it, is one of the biggest reasons to fill positions in our businesses with individuals from this generation.

3. *Millennials are carving a new path in the world.* A Pew social trend study in 2010 found Millennials are confident, connected, and open to change. They are more ethnically and racially diverse than older adults, less religious, and less likely to have served in the military. The survey results showed 61% saying their generation has a unique and distinctive identity. 24% of them say it is because of their use of technology. Only 12% of Gen Xers say technology is a part of its uniqueness. Boomers cite their work ethic at 17%, and the Silent Generation has the

shared experience of WWII which 14% cite as the biggest reason their generation stands apart.

In a recent study it was discovered that 80% of all people do not use their greatest gifts at work. The world is opening to the idea of an empowered, meaningful life as the top priority. Millennials are driving that change. Now the question is, how will we as business leaders respond to the call for change?

Summary

> *"I've learned that people will forget what you said, people will forget what you did, but people will never forget how you made them feel."*
>
> *~ Maya Angelou*

As leaders, it is up to us to create the changes we wish to see and the most effective way to create the change is by engaging each person in our organization on a *human* level. Make people remember how you made them feel, and be sure it is in a positive way. Provide transparency at any opportunity possible in your leadership and ask for people's opinions of how you are doing as a leader. If you are unsure how to do this, contact us and we can come in and help you develop a plan of action.

A new age is upon us. The company organization chart is flattening out and we must adjust accordingly. Leaders must still lead, but we must learn to lead differently than we have been conditioned to by our own generations. We must work twice or three times as hard to bring the younger generations up to speed, and at the same time communicate with them in a way that encourages full engagement and provides a sense of purpose at work that goes beyond a paycheck and a pension plan.

If you have any doubts about what you need to do to do a better job of leading and developing millennial leaders, simply ask one and they will tell you. How you receive and utilize that information may well put you ahead or further behind in retaining your people. Believe me when I say your competitors are working hard to figure out how to attract your best talent away from you. Make it difficult for them... build your plan.

About the Author

Scott Sadler is a Certified Executive Coach, Facilitator, Speaker, Consultant, and an Entrepreneur. He has been a successful business owner for nearly three decades and truly understands the challenges that entrepreneurs face in engaging with the most important and expensive asset in business: human capital.

Having owned businesses that have employed a large number of people as well as consulting with small, medium, and large firms, Scott offers a unique perspective to his clients. His focus is on the people in the business and he believes that all problems in a business ultimately have a communication-based solution.

He is a trusted advisor to companies and individuals all over the country, helping them systemize communication skills that help them understand how to "get to yes" in their daily human engagements. He is **The Millennial Mentor**™ to his clients as they engage generation Y in a positive and profitable way to reduce turnover of this important segment of the workforce in their companies.

Scott lives in the beautiful state of Oregon with his wife Ingrid, pit bull lab mix Austin, and their wild cat, Kimmy. He is an active student of life and his curiosity is never satisfied.

He loves the outdoors and is an experienced mountaineer, backpacker, and wilderness survival student. He and Ingrid enjoy traveling, experiencing different cultures, people, great food, wine, beer, movies, golf, reading, and spending time with friends and family.

CCS
Creative Conflict Solutions

Scott Sadler
creative-conflict-solutions.com